YOUR CHILD'S WELL-BEING - JUVENILE FIBROMYALGIA

A Parent's Guide To Help Your Child or Teenager Manage Home, School & Social Life

CHRISTINE HARRIS & KAY PROTHRO

BALBOA.
PRESS

A DIVISION OF HAY HOUSE

Balboa Press books may be ordered through booksellers or by contacting:

Balboa Press
A Division of Hay House
1663 Liberty Drive
Bloomington, IN 47403
www.balboapress.com
1 (877) 407-4847

Because of the dynamic nature of the Internet, any web addresses or links contained in this book may have changed since publication and may no longer be valid. The views expressed in this work are solely those of the author and do not necessarily reflect the views of the publisher, and the publisher hereby disclaims any responsibility for them.

The author of this book does not dispense medical advice or prescribe the use of any technique as a form of treatment for physical, emotional, or medical problems without the advice of a physician, either directly or indirectly. The intent of the author is only to offer information of a general nature to help you in your quest for emotional and spiritual well-being. In the event you use any of the information in this book for yourself, which is your constitutional right, the author and the publisher assume no responsibility for your actions.

Any people depicted in stock imagery provided by Thinkstock are models, and such images are being used for illustrative purposes only. Certain stock imagery © Thinkstock.

Print information available on the last page.

ISBN: 978-1-5043-3925-4 (sc)
ISBN: 978-1-5043-3926-1 (e)

Balboa Press rev. date: 06/03/2016

CONTENTS

Authors' Foreword

Parents experience an excess of overwhelming feelings and a heightened sense of responsibility whenever a child is ill and hurting. If you are one of these parents, you have probably asked yourself, "Where do I go? What do I need to learn?" The information is out there, yet it may be hard to find. That is why "Your Child's Well–Being" series was created.

Those two questions above are especially relevant if your child is diagnosed with Juvenile Fibromyalgia Syndrome. *Your Child's Well-Being - Juvenile Fibromyalgia* will empower you with basic information and gentle guidance. It is both a private coach, offering advice and helpful techniques, and your "personal cheerleading team," lending resources and strength as you work toward your child's well–being. Each chapter reassures you that the stress of caring for your child is manageable and gets easier over time.

Fibromyalgia Syndrome [FMS] is now a recognized clinical entity causing chronic and disabling pain. There is no medical test one can take that will result in a definitive diagnosis. In fact, it has only been in the last couple of decades that doctors have begun to distinguish this condition from the many easier to diagnose syndromes, such as Depression, Chronic Fatigue Syndrome, Lupus, Multiple Sclerosis, to name a few.

You will not find recommendations for the latest and greatest treatments and/or medications in this book (because we are not doctors and because that sort of information is constantly growing and changing). What you will learn is how to find and access that type of information. You will find out what Fibromyalgia is, what it looks like, and how it is treated by both traditional therapies and holistic approaches to health. As you discover that there are many ways to treat your child, you will hopefully find remedies that work best for you, your child, and your family.

We hope that you will find the information and insights shared here to be of value and comfort. Our job, as the authors of *Your Child's Well-Being - Juvenile Fibromyalgia*, is to help you get to a place where you will find your own direction and gain the strength to advocate for your child and for your family. More importantly, we want to help you keep yourself positive, energized, and centered. We want to help care for you, the parent, so that you can have available as many resources as possible for your child's well–being.

Christine Harris, LCSW, LISW-CP, DCC
Kay Prothro, LCSW–R, ACSW
2015

Note

Because a higher percentage of Fibromyalgia diagnoses occur in girls and women, the authors have chosen to use feminine personal pronouns in referring to your child or teenager throughout this book. (And just so you know, up to 40% of cases have been reported in boys and men.)

Also, we have adopted a more conversational tone, meaning you are not going to find scholarly citations throughout the text. Those sources are included in the body of resources compiled at the end of the book, and we encourage you to seek them out for further information.

Disclaimer

All health–related information appearing in *Your Child's Well-Being - Juvenile Fibromyalgia* is meant for basic informational purposes only. It is not intended to serve as medical advice, substitute for a doctor's consultation or to be used for diagnosing or treating a disease. Readers of this book are advised to consult with their physician(s) or other professional healthcare provider(s) before making any decisions concerning your health and the health of your child. Do not disregard professional medical advice or delay in seeking it because of something you have read in this book. The authors are not responsible for any adverse effects resulting from the use of or reliance on any information contained herein.

CHAPTER 1

START AT THE BEGINNING

You Are Not Alone

We read or hear every day of the many people facing difficult life experiences, especially where a child's well–being is concerned. The most important thing to remember—and possibly the hardest to achieve—is staying positive. Remember that you are not alone. You have a team of doctors and nurse practitioners in your camp. You may even rely on the skills of a nutritionist or an herbalist or an acupuncturist. You are surrounded by a close, caring circle of family, and friends. You and your child will find a workable resolution together, and you will find a greater and stronger sense of yourselves and your family.

As a parent, you become pro–active when it comes to helping your child who is in pain. You will likely have to explore such recognized syndromes and conditions as Depression, Chronic Fatigue Syndrome, Lupus, and Multiple Sclerosis (to name a few) before coming to Juvenile Fibromyalgia Syndrome [JFMS], simply because those symptoms and conditions are far easier to diagnose. Your focus remains on being positive, energized, and centered, never ceasing to find your own direction and strength in order to be an informed advocate for your child and your family.

One pediatric rheumatologist has said that the definition of Fibromyalgia is "full body pain" which causes muscular–skeletal discomfort, fatigue, sleep disturbance, moodiness, and mental fogginess. Fibromyalgia, like other childhood chronic conditions, makes it very difficult for the child to participate in school. For instance, missed school days disrupt the communal continuity of class discussions and lead to a backlog of homework assignments for which your child already has little energy to complete. Having to manage Fibromyalgia on a day–to–day basis also impacts your child's ability to form friendships and participate in age appropriate social activities because her low stamina will not permit her to be as active or stay out as late as the others in her age group. Depending on the degree of severity the child experiences, she can feel very lonely and isolated from her peers, causing depression and anxiety which only feeds into Fibromyalgia flare–ups. (Flare–ups are when all the symptoms are magnified and intensified for a period of time; we write more about flare–ups in Chapter 4.)

At times, your child may feel hopeless and believe her situation will never end. It begins to feel like her life is passing by and nothing ever seems to change. At those times, the child needs an understanding and knowledgeable adult to talk to her and be her support system.

One of the problems with Fibromyalgia is its elusiveness. It's like the Scarlet Pimpernel—"you seek him here, you seek him there, you seek him everywhere." There are certain factors which seem to contribute to the development of Fibromyalgia pain. It is commonly believed by the medical profession that the following characteristics may leave a child more vulnerable to Fibromyalgia:

- sensitivity to pain
- experiencing tremendous stress
- exhibits problems in psychosocial development
- has difficulty in relationships with both family members and peers and/or
- must deal with parents who are challenged by their own life stresses and problems

Most families have a similar beginning experience with Fibromyalgia. The child has repeated bouts of some group of symptoms. Some children experience chronic sore throats, fevers accompanied by fatigue, and body pain. Other children experience sleep problems, extreme fatigue, and feeling emotionally dispirited. Symptoms can repeat over time and can occur in various combinations that may show up differently with each flare–up.

General practitioners (GPs) and pediatricians do their best to treat the symptoms. When the treatment does not result in long term success [meaning a long period of wellness], they will usually start referring the patient to a specialist. Often the ear, nose, and throat consultant is called in to make further assessment. Other times a referral to a neurologist is made. Many families report that by the time a diagnosis of Juvenile Fibromyalgia is made, their child has been assessed by three to five physicians.

Generally, until a child is about twelve years old, she will not be given a diagnosis of Juvenile Fibromyalgia but instead the description of their symptoms will include the words "myofascial pain" rather than a formal diagnosis. This might be because physicians tend to err on the side of caution rather than prematurely diagnose.

DOES YOUR CHILD HAVE A DIAGNOSIS?

Until a formal diagnosis has been made, your child's treatment and school life may be as chaotic as the symptoms she is having. It is a good idea to involve everyone who deals with your child, and keep them involved by talking openly and honestly about her situation. Let them know that you are looking for their support and cooperation. Keep track on your family planning calendar if your child is missing days of school or practice sessions in her after school activities. This is important information that will be helpful either to health practitioners and/or the school in the future.

Figuring out what is happening to your child if you do not have a confirmed diagnosis, or even if you do, is one of the frustrating elements of Fibromyalgia because the symptoms vary from person to person. The treatment approaches vary. The medications are varied. The alternative healthcare options are extremely varied.

HOW TO TALK OPENLY ABOUT YOUR CHILD'S DIAGNOSIS

It does not help that most people do not seem to know exactly what Fibromyalgia is. You may find yourself constantly explaining when you are met with the question, "She has Fibro–What?" Or "Yeah, I think I heard something about that. What is it again?" Suggestion: keep your explanation simple. It takes energy from you to provide the explanation. You need to pace yourself for your own sake and for that of your child and your family.

Adopting and repeating the same, simple explanation is an energy–saving way to explain Fibromyalgia to others. The phrase, "full body pain," is something that most people will easily be able to understand. And it is pretty much how the American College of Rheumatology (ACR) defines Fibromyalgia. Their definition of Fibromyalgia has been updated. The first definition involved an examination of eighteen specific tender points in the human body. The ACR required evidence of body pain in a minimum of eleven points. Susmita Kashikar-Zuck, Ph.D., Professor of Pediatrics at The Cincinnati Children's Medical Center says, "The American College of Rheumatology guidelines no longer require a tender point exam. The widespread pain in many body areas and associated symptoms of ongoing fatigue, sleep disturbance, and cognitive difficulties is enough to give the diagnosis once other potential medical causes are ruled out." About the only other piece of information you might want to add is that "the symptoms come and go." This is a simple explanation that will save you from having to discuss too many details.

FEELINGS ABOUT THE DIAGNOSIS OF FIBROMYALGIA

It is normal to experience a variety of feelings after your child or teen has been diagnosed with Fibromyalgia. You may feel angry, go into denial, feel sad or scared or frustrated. All this and more is normal because you are in the midst of feeling grief over the loss of your expectations as well as the uncertainty of what your child will have to endure. Most parents expect that life will throw their child challenges here and there and that the child will grow up to be a fully independent adult with the help and guidance that a loving parent can provide. The diagnosis of Fibromyalgia or any serious condition may send you into a spiral of grief.

The grief process will be easier if you are gentle with yourself and allow yourself a safe place to express your feelings. Writing your feelings in a journal or diary, reaching out to supportive friends, family, counselors, and spiritual teachers, are all good ways of working through the different feelings that will come up for you. There are many support groups available, and the Internet is an easy way to find them. There are groups to be found on the Internet at Meetup.com, as well as many social media groups via Facebook, etc. (See Appendix for additional resources.) Your community and/or hospital center may also have local support groups.

Remember that your child is going to react to how you are feeling. Therefore, working through your own feelings on your own time is a priority. Trying to be stoic is not going to help you or your child. Working through your feelings is important because children easily pick up on parents' moods and feelings, and they need the best from you at a time like this.

Building a Stronger "You"

Being a parent requires strength, the full body kind, not just being emotionally strong. It is in everyone's interest that you increase your strength. By becoming physically strong, you will increase the energy needed to help yourself and your child. Your endorphin levels will increase, and increased endorphins will help fend off the emotional dips which are a natural part of the Fibromyalgia territory for both parent and child. Working out, cycling, Pilates, yoga, Tai Ch, or just getting your heart rate up for 20 minutes every other day will help you balance your mood and your energy. Your patience will increase. And (from a mental health point of view) you will be expressing your feelings and thoughts via your body.

Building a stronger "you" can be very simple and affordable. Walk up and down a set of stairs. Run in place. Ride a bicycle. Shoot hoops or play volleyball with the neighbors in your back yard.

Dance. The list of what you might be doing to bring your heart rate up is endless. Of course, if you have medical issues, you will need to consult your healthcare provider before you embark on any fitness program. The point is that since you are your child's primary caregiver, you will need to take care of yourself first. As is so often mentioned, this is the part of your journey where you need to put the oxygen mask over your own face first and then your child's (as in an airplane). It is really important that you care for yourself as if you were the best parent for yourself.

CHAPTER 2

WHAT YOUR DOCTORS WILL TELL YOU

Learning the Ins and Outs

WHAT IS IT?

Fibromyalgia in children and teenagers is commonly referred to as Juvenile Fibromyalgia Syndrome [JFMS] or Juvenile Primary Fibromyalgia Syndrome [JPFS]. It is a diagnosis which falls into the category of rheumatic conditions like arthritis. Rheumatologists deal mostly with arthritis–related conditions; however, Fibromyalgia is different from an arthritis–related condition. Arthritis is a disease of the joints caused by inflammation which can cause damage to muscle, joint, and tissue. Fibromyalgia Syndrome is a condition considered to be a pain syndrome that is chronic and generalized.

Fibromyalgia is a variety of symptoms that take the shape of overall pain and fatigue. Symptoms may include: overall pain in the body; fogginess in thinking (nicknamed "fibro fog" due to one's less than optimal cognitive function); low and/or anxious moods; fatigue; lack of good sleep and/or waking up refreshed; stomach and digestion issues; and/or sensitivity to temperature.

Your child or teenager may also experience painful menstrual cycles and more severe acne.

Your child or teenager may currently have or previously have had some of these symptoms. You should be aware that symptoms may come and go and may change over time. In general, your child may expect to experience similar symptoms in adulthood. As Fibromyalgia research grows, more and more awareness of symptoms will be better understood and known and, hopefully, make day–to–day living easier for your child.

WHO GETS FIBROMYALGIA?

There seem to be some children or teenagers who have a particular group of experiences and/or backgrounds which are also found in adults diagnosed with Fibromyalgia. Genetic research is beginning to show that Fibromyalgia might be passed down through familial generations. Some patients who develop Fibromyalgia have reported experiencing high periods of stress and/or being involved in a serious accident. Others who have recovered from a serious illness, like mononucleosis or an especially strong influenza, have later received a diagnosis of Fibromyalgia. In still others, Fibromyalgia seems to develop gradually over a long period of time or else it may come on suddenly. There is no clear cut answer as to who gets Fibromyalgia or why they get it.

HOW IS FIBROMYALGIA DIAGNOSED?
WHAT ARE THE CAUSES?

Doctors, whether they be GPs, pediatricians, or pediatric rheumatologists, may diagnose Fibromyalgia. They first need to rule out rheumatic disease as well as other pain–related diagnoses.

There is no specific testing available as yet for Fibromyalgia, like a blood test, an EEG, or an EKG. Rather, the physician will look for the features of wide-spread pain and other symptoms like fatigue, poor sleep, and cognitive difficulties as Dr. Kashikar-Zuck previously described.

For the child or teenager, the prominent feature of Fibromyalgia is generally pain. Research indicates that how pain is experienced is an important indicator in Fibromyalgia. Several factors create the person's pain experience and must be taken into account. Stress levels, emotional distress, the parents' history regarding pain, family history of physical and psychological pain, plus understanding the family's ability to function as a unit, are all factors.

The psychological aspects of pain are not the only factors being considered by the doctor. More and more researchers are examining how the patient's body interprets pain. Some research studies now are seeking to understand if the pain is enhanced because of "abnormal sensory processing in the person's central nervous system." One such study focused on central sensitivity syndromes, a new paradigm and group classification for Fibromyalgia and overlapping conditions, and the related issue of disease versus illness. As a result of such investigations it is generally thought that the Fibromyalgia body is far more sensitive to pain.

Eileen R Giardino, RN, MSN, PhD, FNP-BC, ANP-BC, has written that JPFS is on the rise in the juvenile population, resulting in more and more research being conducted (notably at the Department of Pediatrics, Yokohama City University School of Medicine, Yokohama, Japan). Some sources say that there are 10,000 new cases of JPFS in the United States each year. The Childrens' Hospital of Philadelphia reports that approximately 2%–4% of the juvenile population has the JPFS diagnosis. The

Icelandic medical journal, **Laeknabladid**, reports percentages as high as 7% of the juvenile population. (Bear in mind that statistics should be taken with a grain of salt. Their validity is determined by the particular type of statistical analysis and research protocols employed.)

There is over a decade's worth of research coming out of Susmita Kashikar-Zuck's Lab which is tackling many facets of Fibromyalgia – psychological; how CBT is used with it; what recipe of exercise and CBT might be helpful to teenagers; and even studying the parents of Fibromyalgia kids! Dr. Kashikar-Zuck's work is based in the area of pediatric pain research.

The good news in Fibromyalgia research and its prognosis with children and teenagers is that there appears to be a more frequent return to wellness because children and teenagers are still growing and developing. Published clinical studies indicate that 60% of those diagnosed with JPFS eventually return to normal functioning.

How Is Fibromyalgia Treated?

There are several ways that physicians will want to treat Fibromyalgia. They will want to help the patient to both manage her pain and be better able to manage her energy levels. This boils down to focusing on the areas of pain management, sleep hygiene, and exercise.

Medication and Pain Management

When it comes to pain, the Food and Drug Administration (FDA) in the United States is the governmental body which approves medications. At this writing there are at least three medications approved by the FDA to treat pain in Fibromyalgia. They are milnacipran, duloxetine, and pregabalin.

Milnacipran is commonly known in America as Savella and is the most recently FDA approved medication for Fibromyalgia. Savella's original use was for depression and now has been found sometimes to be helpful with neuropathic pain and Fibromyalgia in adults.

Duloxetine is commonly known as Cymbalta and is often used as an anti–depressant. It has also been found to help in relieving Fibromyalgia pain. The FDA approved Cymbalta for treating chronic musculoskeletal pain in 2008.

Pregabalin is known on both sides of the Atlantic as Lyrica. The drug works by reducing the ability of nerves to send pain messages to each other. It was approved for Fibromyalgia patients by the FDA in 2007.

Be aware that these medications do not work well with certain nutritional supplements such as Tryptophan and 5–HTP. It is always wise to tell each and every one of your health practitioners what medications and supplements—both over the counter and prescription—your child or teenager is currently taking. Also communicate what adverse effects, if any, your child felt from previous medications or supplements. The website MedlinePlus (http://www.nlm.nih.gov/medlineplus/) is a reliable source for information regarding medications.

The group of over–the–counter medications known as the NSAIDs, which stands for non–steroidal anti–inflammatory drugs, is made up of anti–inflammatory medicines such as ibuprofen (Advil or Nurofen), aspirin, and naproxen (Naprosyn or Aleve). While the NSAIDs do relieve pain, be aware that there are trade–offs in the form of side effects. Prolonged use of NSAIDS, for example, can be tough on the stomach and the kidneys and liver.

All medication should be monitored on a regular basis for its effectiveness and side effects. Ask your pharmacist and physician how much time your child is expected to need before the full effect of the prescribed medication becomes apparent. Also ask how long your child should be taking any particular medication. It is generally a good idea to review what medications are being used every few months. Are the medications helping or not, and what are their long term effects? Again, use your common sense when it comes to your child taking medications. Remember, too, that although medications were invented for good reasons, these drugs are going to be used on a young, growing body. Caution is advised, and most physicians will be conservative if they determine that prescribing a medication is in the best interest of the patient.

<u>Sleep Hygiene</u>

Fibromyalgia may interfere with your child or teenager's ability to go to sleep, and her pain level during the night may cause her to wake up. Taking the time to learn something about the mechanism of sleep will help make her sleep hygiene more manageable and possible.

Napping may be a temptation after your child or teenager has had a rough night and did not get her required amount of sleep. You should encourage her to resist napping as much as possible because it will most likely upset her nightly sleep cycle. Resting is OK, but make sure that your child or teenager does not fall asleep, especially if she is resting in her bed. Just being on her bed will subconsciously trigger her "sleep" mode, so it is a good idea to check periodically that she doesn't fall asleep outside of her sleep cycle.

Getting ready to go to sleep is about making a structure that will be easy and will be welcoming. She should first do the physical tasks, such as getting out her clothes for the next day, organizing her school books, tidying the bedroom, brushing her teeth, washing her face, and taking a bath. In the few hours before bed, she should avoid caffeinated drinks, hot drinks, and exercise. Exercising after dinner will likely prove too stimulating and make it more difficult for her to fall asleep after she's in bed.

For the next stage of inviting sleep, there needs to be a ritual "settling down." For example, she might listen to a calming CD or read a few pages of a book. The bedroom temperature should be slightly cool and the lights out. If a night light is needed, place it where the beam is not within a direct line of sight from the bed. She will need to keep all stimuli to a minimum at this time. It is also important to stick to a regular bedtime, even on weekends or during vacations.

Once she is ready to go to sleep, your daughter needs to settle into a comfortable position under the covers. Perhaps she will need extra pillows to support her legs or arms. Encourage her to pick her sleep position carefully and not to move around very much. Shifting positions while going to sleep may seem natural, but for your child or teen, every adjustment becomes a signal to the brain that she wants to wake up. Tossing and turning does not help her at all; it just makes her situation worse when sleep is the desired goal.

The Mayo Clinic and many pediatric rheumatologists advise that medication may be helpful with regulating sleep patterns and make it easier to fall asleep. One such medication is Elavil (also known as Amitriptyline). It is prescribed when your child's sleep patterns become disturbed and leave her chronically drowsy and fatigued to the degree that mental acuity is diminished. The drug works by increasing the amounts of certain natural substances in the brain that are needed to maintain mental balance.

Another tip is to use the "yoga breath" to fall asleep. The yoga breath is a four–count breath made up of inhaling to the count of four . . . holding the breath for two counts . . . exhaling to the count of four . . . holding the breath for two counts . . . and repeat again and again until asleep. This breathing technique is like a meditation as well, and it serves as a focus to distract the mind from being so aware of thoughts and/or feelings of pain or discomfort. [Additional relaxation techniques are discussed in Chapter 3.]

Exercise

Moderate exercise will help with many aspects of Fibromyalgia. Such exercises help with mood and physical flexibility. Learning how much to do, when to do it, and for how long, will be an individual choice. Finding the right balance is going to require a bit of experimentation. Physical therapists who have extensive experience with Fibromyalgia are familiar with a variety of exercises that are simple and effective in helping to relieve pain. Physical therapists working with your child or teenager need to have had training with Fibromyalgia patients. If they have not, they may push your child too hard which might cause her to experience a Fibromyalgia flare–up.

While your child or teenager may have participated in basketball, football, and other sports, it may be time to readjust her form of exercise. Tai Chi, yoga, stretching exercises, and other types of exercise like Pilates, may be an easier way to get her into a regular exercise regimen. Many physicians will suggest that she exercise multiple times during the week, perhaps even every day.

It is best to start out small. A five–minute workout routine is a good beginning foundation. Her two goals in exercising should be consistency and slowly increasing the duration of her workout time to 20–30 minutes. The main thing is to keep her exercise routine fun. You may find that it will help your child's motivation if you workout with her— a very good thing for yourself, as you will be relieving your own stress, and strengthening your body while supporting and motivating your child or teen.

What you must watch out for when it comes to an exercise routine is that it does not raise your child's level of fatigue or increase her pain and stiffness. That is why avoiding strenuous exercise and slowly increasing the amount of time she exercises is important. And if your child is experiencing a flare–up, it would be better to stop exercising until the flare–up has passed. More helpful would be coaching your child to breathe through her pain or discomfort with any number of breathing techniques.

Another benefit of regular exercise is that it will improve your child or teenager's sense of her own power and confidence. It will also boost her self–esteem. Remember that the benefits of exercise are cumulative—the more she sticks with it, even at five minutes per session, the greater the improvement she will begin to notice. Exercise is a great activity for feeling empowered and having some sort of self control when living with so unpredictable a syndrome as Fibromyalgia.

COUNSELING

Fibromyalgia may affect mood, and you may realize in hindsight that your child's mood was already low or anxious prior to getting the JFMS diagnosis. Counseling is often introduced into her routine as a way to help her gain skills to lift her mood. The psychological theory of Cognitive Behavioral Therapy (CBT) is often the approach recommended by rheumatologists or other health practitioners. Through CBT, your child will learn how to understand her thought patterns and her environment in a more positive way. Once your child has mastered CBT, it is easier for her to make "lemonade out of lemons"—i.e., turn the negative into a positive.

Counseling also creates a space for your child to heal any past crisis or trauma or stress that she has not yet fully understood or digested. Family Therapy provides a safe place for the whole family to come to terms with how Fibromyalgia impacts the family. You, the parents, may decide to enter into couples counseling in order to strengthen your personal bond and strengthen communication skills. Counseling helps you maintain a positive attitude as you are adapting to the changes that Fibromyalgia demands on both you and the family unit.

CHAPTER 3

MAINSTREAM MEDICAL TREATMENTS AREN'T YOUR ONLY OPTIONS

Complementary Approaches & Integrative Medicine

◆

COMMON SENSE

Remember to trust your common sense. Remember also to "go with your gut" as you apply your common sense to various suggestions. Fibromyalgia is a chronic syndrome that is uniquely felt by each person that it affects. What may work for one person might not work for another. Or, it might work one time but not the next. And if you come across an approach that you feel is too unconventional, do not pursue it. For parents of a child with Fibromyalgia, it's important that common sense rule over fatigue, panic, and/or frustration—feelings that come with the territory of raising a child who has a chronic syndrome.

This section is an introduction to some alternative resources which have proven effective for some children and teenagers living with Fibromyalgia. While there seems to be an infinite array of things to do for your child in the land of alternative healthcare, you need to exercise common sense around what your child or teenager is exposed to in your effort to help her live more comfortably.

"Integrative medicine" and "alternative medicines" are terms which cover a wide range of treatments used in the health and well–being field. There is no one particular definition for these terms. "Evidenced–based" is another phrase you may hear that is used both in Western medicine and in the integrative medicine world. Evidence–based simply means that there is statistical research to back up or disprove a procedure, treatment or approach.

In America, the National Institutes of Complementary and Alternative Medicine (NICAM), a branch of the National Institutes of Health (NIH), is a respected source of thoroughly researched information regarding various procedures. There are also many institutes, foundations, and associations around the globe which research integrative and alternative medicine. And there is the Internet—but beware, as the Internet is a very broad but thin tool and must be used in a thoughtful way. If you have ever taken a course in research methods, you will already know how to navigate and trawl through the information on the Internet. And if you do not have that sort of training, you may need a bit of guidance about which sites to trust and which ones will require caution. See Appendix for resources.

THE KITCHEN SINK APPROACH

In the beginning stages of managing JFMS, you will most likely adopt the "Kitchen Sink" approach—trying anything and everything you learn hoping it will help. How you treat your child's diet, lifestyle, and physical body are but a few of the areas you might explore.

Massage, for instance, has been said to help and ease the tension and spasms in muscles. Acupuncture and Chinese herbal medicine have been around for thousands of years and have been shown to be effective in working with Fibromyalgia pain. Nutritional supplements and whole foods are also important and can offer much needed relief.

The Pediatric Rheumatologist will most likely recommend a prescribed exercise regime that suits your child's current state of Fibromyalgia. This prescription may be the only step the rheumatologist makes. Meanwhile you are living with a person who is in pain, discomfort, and not living life as her best self by any stretch of the imagination.

Your child or teen may also be prescribed medications that—fingers crossed—will reduce her symptoms. As Western medicine is all about diagnosis and the reduction of symptoms, the root of the problem is sometimes not resolved. Therefore, medication may be ongoing and eventually result in further side effects. While your child may or may not experience side effects, be aware they can occur. On that cautionary note, it is wise to go about finding thoughtful ways of assisting your child's body to metabolize and digest these medications.

If you choose to enter the world of alternative and integrative medicines, the caution here is that Western medical personnel are generally not trained in integrative, alternative, and energetic medicine and so do not know what will happen when pharmaceutical products are mixed with herbs. It is very important that whoever you are consulting with in fields outside of Western medicine, is someone who is up to date on how your child's medicine interacts with alternative remedies.

Looking to other ways of helping your child is normal. Just be methodical and write down what you are doing when you start something new, and what you notice in the way of changes. And of course, if there is an adverse reaction, contact your primary care physician. Always keep your doctor(s) in the loop. If you are not communicating with your child's medical team, you will be getting in the way of your child's care. Plus, you will be setting a poor example for your child who knows exactly what you are doing with her. It is also important that she learns to be honest with her healthcare providers because at a future date she will be own advocate.

Your child or teenager's healthcare practitioners may not like what you tell them regarding the alternatives to their recommended treatment plan. However, you are educating them as well as being honest with them concerning their patient. Good medical practitioners will be honest about their lack of information concerning chiropractic care or acupuncture, for example. They should, however, be willing to hear you out and want to hear how whatever you are adding to your child's regimen for good health is working for your child. Fibromyalgia treatment is still in its infancy. So whatever you add to the clinical picture concerning your child is a plus for her medical team.

MASSAGE THERAPY

The massage therapist needs to be someone who has a lot of experience working on clients who have Fibromyalgia or other forms of chronic pain. If you do not have a personal referral, contact organizations that certify and track bona fide massage therapists and ask who is available in your area.

The American Massage Therapy Association provides a registry for massage therapists as well as a therapist locator. Profiles of their members will also include whether or not they have training and experience with Fibromyalgia. See Appendix.

There is also the National Certification Board for Therapeutic Massage and Bodywork in which all American massage therapists need to be licensed. In America, each state establishes the regulations for the basic licenses and certifications that massage therapists must hold in order to practice, and those required credentials will vary from state to state. Each state will have a website where one may verify that a massage therapist is licensed, board certified, and a member in good standing. See Appendix.

Word of mouth is the best referral source since the person you seek has already been "tested" by the trusted friend who gave you the referral. Once you have the referral, your next question should be, is this therapist "good enough" for my child? Unless you were given the referral by someone who is currently or has been that therapist's client, the best way to know if the massage therapist is the right one for your child is by getting a massage from that therapist yourself.

Checking out any healthcare practitioner yourself will help save your child from feeling very bounced around. Also, the information that you provide to the practitioners is valuable and helps them to get a head start on where to begin with your child.

Finally, a good massage is a wonderful thing for anyone, especially for your child or teenager. It is an hour of deep relaxation–finally. A good massage will benefit your child for the next two to three days and provide a welcome break for her.

ACUPUNCTURE

Acupuncture comes to Western culture from a tradition of Oriental Medicine said to be 3,000 plus years old. It has been well documented as a complete healthcare system by NICAM and the World Health Organization (WHO). Acupuncture can be applied to all aspects of Fibromyalgia including the roots of the disorder.

Acupuncture approaches patients from their own unique perspective, i.e., each individual is different. In Chinese medicine, this is called "pattern discrimination." The acupuncturist uses a protocol that investigates patients from the point of view of four different examinations in order to come up with the prescribed treatment. This is different from the Western medical model which relies upon the patients' diagnosis, and which ultimately treats all patients in the same manner as per the protocol of the particular disease or disorder. Ultimately what this means, for example, is that two children or teenagers, both diagnosed with Fibromyalgia, would be treated differently based on the difference in their Chinese patterns. (Western medicine would treat them exactly the same.) This is a simplified explanation of Chinese medicine which includes acupuncture along with other modalities such as herbal medicines.

Once again a personal referral may be the best way to find a good acupuncturist who is credentialed and licensed in your area. Each state in America and each country in Europe have their own local medical board that license acupuncturists. In America, the National Certification Commission for Acupuncture and Oriental Medicine is the nationally recognized association certifying acupuncturists. In Europe, there is the European Traditional Chinese Medical Association. The Traditional Chinese Medicine Resource Center provides a listing of local and national acupuncture organizations in the U.S. as well as international organizations and acupuncture regulation sites worldwide.

Acupuncturists are sometimes found in hospitals in the Integrative Medicine Department. More commonly, they are either working in their own private practices or in community acupuncture clinics. Fees in a private practice setting are usually higher per session than a community acupuncture clinic offering services on a sliding scale fee structure. The People's Organization of Community Acupuncture in the U.S. provides information on finding a clinic. In Europe, the Association of Community and Multibed Acupuncture Clinics provide the same service. What makes community acupuncture different from private practice acupuncture is that patients are treated together in the same room. The ethos is that the more affordable treatment is, the patient will come more frequently for treatments and thus the quicker they will progress.

What can you expect from the experience of acupuncture? The hair–thin sterile needles that are inserted by the acupuncturist may cause a sensation or prick or something like a mosquito bite. This sensation dissipates within seconds. The treatment session is usually about 30 to 60 minutes long depending on the person and the condition being treated. Many people sleep during their treatments and feel energized or extremely relaxed afterwards. Acupuncture usually requires a series of sessions at the outset to be effective, and later on appointments are spaced out to a maintenance level once relief has been gained. Acupuncture can be used to treat practically all medical conditions.

EMOTIONAL FREEDOM TECHNIQUE (EFT)

EFT, also known as Tapping, is a method which was first developed by Roger Callahan and later adapted into current practice by Gary Craig. This technique involves repetitively tapping seven points on the face and upper torso gently with the fingertips while repeating short sentences that the instructor or the person makes up as they are tapping. The tapped points (lightly, with the person's own two fingers) are acupressure points. The method draws on a cognitive behavioral approach to change the way the brain makes sense of bothersome thoughts or behaviors. Because Tapping is based on acupuncture principles, it also has been clinically proven to lower stress as it brings down cortisol levels in the body. It is an easy method to help your child or teenager to change her thinking about pain, frustration, and depression. Tapping also happens to be fun when approached in a light–hearted way because it is like playing a game. Brad Yates, a leading expert on Tapping, uses EFT to help people release negative attitudes. He is the author of many books and has a large free video collection on Youtube. com. He also has a book for children which is fun and effective called *The Wizard's Wish*. See Appendix.

BECOMING CALM

Living with Fibromyalgia is a constant source of stress for you, the parent, and for your child. Some days will be better than others, but how do you help your child cope with that stress? Additionally, how do you cope with that stress? The subject of stress and its effects has become an area that is heavily researched and documented. There are many approaches to easing stress levels such as mindfulness meditation and autogenic relaxation. Rather than overwhelm you with a long list of techniques, we offer here a few very simple techniques to get you started in learning how to decrease stress levels.

A quick and easy way is for both of you and your child to carve out a little "me" time, a sort of mini–vacation from the ups and downs of daily life. During your "me" time, the goal is to set aside all thoughts about your cares and worries and fears. To help you do that, there are a few simple techniques that may help you find the space to let go of your anxieties and become "calm." Or at least more calm.

You will likely want to be sitting when you try these techniques. In general, just sit up straight. Your eyes may be open or closed, and let your hands rest comfortably on your thighs.

<u>Breathing</u>

Breathing techniques are just about the easiest to learn and practice. You can do them anytime, anywhere, and they only require a quiet place to sit. Try this:

> Sit comfortably with your eyes closed. Now, exhale. When you arrive at the end of the exhalation, count "one." Now inhale slowly, and when you have fully inflated your lungs, count "two." Repeat these steps for several minutes or as long as you like. When you are ready to end this practice, just be aware of how calm you feel and carry that feeling with you as you resume your activities.

Visualizations

Visualizations are a useful tool because they quickly allow us to step out of our stressful, everyday lives, and step into a serene space where everything is calm and still and abundant. This visualization, commonly known as *Blue Sky*, is a good example:

> Sit or lie down for this one. Picture a beautiful blue sky without any clouds in it. As you focus on the sky, feel your body growing lighter and lighter. Close your eyes and hold the image of the sky in your mind. Remember that the sky is empty and endless, spreading out in every direction with no beginning and no end. Begin to feel your body get even lighter and lighter until you have floated up into your clear blue sky. See yourself floating there, and let all tension, fatigue, worry, and problems you have just fall away back down to the ground. Relax your mind and allow your breathing its own steady rhythm. Feel yourself gently drifting like a kite in this clear, endless sky. Begin to notice your thoughts slowing down. Feel your entire body merging with the peace and tranquility of that blue sky until you have actually become your clear blue sky. Experience your body and mind as having dissolved away in this infinite, limitless blue sky. You have become the perfect peace and tranquility of the blue sky. Completely let go and just experience "bliss" for as long as you wish. When you are ready, open your eyes. Pay attention to the sense of peace, relaxation, and poise you have generated. Allow this renewal of energy, joy, and calm to stay with you as you go about the rest of your day.

Gazing

The last technique we are introducing here is *gazing*. In this practice, you pick an object and softly allow your eyes to take in everything about it while sitting in your meditation posture. This object can be anything—a marble, a candle flame, a single flower, a flower arrangement, a tree, or any object that gives you joy or holds some special meaning for you.

Begin the practice by placing your object a short distance in front of you and slightly below your face. Start your soft-eyed gaze at the center point of your object and let your eyes gently roam over every part of your object by moving them in a clockwise spiral motion. Dismiss all thoughts you may have about your object and experience it as it is in this moment. If you happen to be outdoors gazing at a tree, for example, notice how the leaves yield to the gentle wind. If you are gazing at a flower arrangement, focus your gaze on the shadows rather than the bright colors. Or focus on the very brightest hues and ignore the shadows. You make the choice.

Practice for at least five minutes or so. Allow the activity to reach deeper and deeper into your mind. Find there a profound sense of calm, inner peace, spiritual connection, and carry it into the remainder of your day.

YOGA

Bridie Hackett, a Satyananda Yoga Teacher in Ireland, has said ". . . yoga helps people move into their own body and reclaim who they are. The most important thing about yoga is that it stops the stress . . . and they can come home to themselves and finally rest."

Yoga is 5,000 years old, comes from India and involves the breath, the body, and meditation. It has become more and more popular over the last century, first in Europe, and then spreading to the Americas. Today there are many different yoga practices all of which can trace their lineage back thousands of years. Some of the ones you may have read about are Hatha, Ashtanga, Bikram, Iyengar, Hot Yoga, and a modern version called Strala Yoga.

One of yoga's brilliant features is that it may be practiced by anyone who has the ability to be aware of his or her own body. So no matter what the challenge, disability, or illness, each person is able to practice some form of yoga. This means that it is an excellent way to help your child or teen when she is feeling Fibromyalgia symptoms. It is a way to increase her physical and mental resilience and strength as well.

Here is one yoga technique that should be easy for your child to practice and may bring her some relief. It comes from the ancient Satyananda Yoga style which is well known for gentle postures. This technique focuses on bringing the breath more deeply into the body. What this practice achieves is help in removing stale oxygen out of the lungs, relaxing the body and increasing a sense of power and control.

Take a normal breath, breathing in, and breathing out. After the next inhalation, take another inhalation. This second inhalation does not have to be a big inhale. Whatever you are capable of doing is perfect. Just follow and repeat the rhythm: *inhale, exhale, inhale, inhale, exhale; inhale, exhale, inhale, inhale, exhale.* And that's it . . . pretty simple, right? Try practicing *inhale, exhale, inhale, inhale, exhale* and notice what your body feels. Remember: "Easy does it." Keep this and all yoga practices gentle . . . no stress or strain allowed!

CHAPTER 4

YOU KNOW YOUR CHILD

Balancing Home, Life, and School

◆

EASING YOUR CHILD'S PAIN AND SORENESS

You will recognize and become aware of the signals your child starts to get when she begins showing symptoms of Fibromyalgia pain and soreness. Through trial and error you will come up with a set of workable pain management skills that make her more comfortable than others. Think of those skills as your "toolbox" and be ready to use one of those tools when her flare–ups occur and pain or soreness moves throughout her body.

A flare–up refers to symptoms that have come back or an indication that stronger symptoms are developing. Her body will signal the onset of a flare–up, and how a flare–up appears will vary for everyone. She could feel a chill, or run a slight fever. She may say she has a headache, feels like her brain is in a fog, or that her bones ache. These are just some of the common symptoms that may indicate the onset of a flare–up.

Once your child senses a flare–up coming on, it is time to reach into your carefully assembled toolbox and use one of those tools. For instance, your child might get into bed and just rest. She might lie in bed and listen to a guided meditation. Another tool may be catering her diet; for example, see that she does not consume sugar that day. Some teens have noticed feeling better after a massage or an acupuncture treatment. These are by no means the only tools. You and your child or teen are going to discover all sorts of additional tools. You are going to put them in that toolbox, and you are going to use them when necessary.

With experience you and your child will have a series of "go to" tools that specifically help her. As she uses the tools, your child will report that her energy is better, her brain is not as foggy, and that her body is less achy. These are possible signs that the flare–up is diminishing.

TALKING WITH YOUR CHILD

By now you have probably taken care of your child many times when she was sick. You know if she is the sort of child who is quiet, clingy, agitated or whiney when she is ill. Each child has her own manner of being a sick person.

Something that the medical professionals understand as well as you, the parent, is that the child's "self-report" is limited. What she says is rarely as detailed as her doctor is accustomed to hearing. How she describes what she's feeling is limited by her age. Not only is the self-report limited by how verbal the child is, but also when it comes to talking to you, she may offer only limited information. On an unconscious level, she may feel that she needs to protect you. Sometimes children, especially ones with chronic illnesses, are very tuned into a parent's moods and may feel like they are a burden.

How to Talk About Her Health

Parents bombard children with directions, questions, and long explanations in an effort to understand what is happening with them. Too much talking is tough on any child, especially one who is hurting or in discomfort. You may find yourself asking questions like, "How do your arms and legs feel? Are you dizzy? Do you still have a headache? Where does it hurt?" Remember that timing is everything.

You know when your child is able to answer your questions easily. Limit asking questions to a time when she is in the mood to talk. When you do talk with her, ask her to describe what she is feeling and help her with descriptive words like "sharp, squishy, hot, cold, achy, etc." One technique to make talking about your child's health easier is getting her to imagine what it would be like if it were her pet who was feeling what she is, or perhaps a cartoon figure. This technique helps her to detach a bit and may give you a more thorough description of what is going on with her.

When you are talking to your child about her symptoms, a good rule of thumb is to limit the length of your conversation to one minute per year of her age. This is especially important when you have important questions or need to impress upon her a specific point. For example, with a ten year old you talk for only ten minutes at a time; with your fifteen year old you have fifteen minutes to get your points across or ask your questions.

It is also important to be mindful and respectful of your child whenever you are in front of a health practitioner. Put yourself in her shoes. Most health practitioners are well trained in talking to your child and are able to elicit a good amount of information from a patient. Let them do their job and fill in the gaps at the end of the appointment or when there is an appropriate break in the conversation.

No matter your child's age, it is important that she feels empowered in her own healthcare. Fibromyalgia is a chronic condition that requires time and self management. The earlier she is able to develop skills to care and advocate for herself, the better.

How to Talk About Pain

How you think and talk about pain will directly impact how your child manages the pain. Perhaps she says something like, "My elbow hurts so much it is killing me." And perhaps you automatically reply, "It can't be killing you."

What that type of remark does is diminishes her real feeling at that moment. A better response would be to help her "reframe" the context of temporary pain by gently guiding her into separating herself from that pain: "It sounds like your elbow is in so much pain that it's not even alive." The reframed sentence says the exact same thing, only it substitutes the more positive word, "alive," for a non–positive one, "killing." Depending upon your child's tone, it might offer you an opportunity to make a joke about the "alive elbow." The object here becomes helping her detach from the pain by changing her focus.

As we mentioned earlier, children and teens express pain in different ways. Some suffer in silence. Some have trouble communicating exactly what the pain is and how it makes them feel. And some have absolutely no difficulty letting you know how they feel.

Gently encourage your child to voice any pain. The very act of describing what or how she is feeling enables her to express pain, and her ability to discuss the pain will help her heal. However, it is important to find a balance between expressing pain and repeatedly talking about it over and over. If an obsession with the pain develops, it can then become "bigger" and "go deeper" into her body.

The next point to be aware of is how she speaks about pain and the importance of reminding her that the pain is only a small part of her. Detachment or "distancing" is a learned skill in pain management. It is the ability to look at a problem—in this instance, the pain—from a distance. This technique helps create the space for your child to gain a bigger perspective and not feel so overwhelmed with the pain.

One way of practicing detachment is making a conscious effort not to say, "my pain" or "your pain." Just replace the personal pronouns with "the pain." Granted you will need to be diplomatic teaching and modeling this change in language. This is a well–regarded form of Cognitive Behavioral Therapy (CBT) and effectively helps create distance between the person and the pain.

For more in depth information regarding pain management please refer to **Conquering Your Child's Chronic Pain: A Pediatrician's Guide for Reclaiming a Normal Childhood**, by Lonnie K. Zeltzer, M.D. and Christina Blackett Schlank.

STAYING ONE STEP AHEAD

One aspect of your job is to ally yourself with your child's practitioners. For now, it is helpful to realize that having a child living with Fibromyalgia means that you will need to look upon this as a part–time job. This is a job that will become smaller and smaller as you find your way and figure out the right "mix" that helps your child.

Part of that management process will require taking the time to look at your schedule regarding your other children, your work, and your personal life. Start simplifying your schedule in whatever ways you are able because you are going to need the extra time to get up to speed on Fibromyalgia. Think mind, body, spirit. Look at all parts of your child's life and see what help is available. Look at your family life, and see how the pieces need to work together.

A good first step is calling in your "Senior Parents." These are your friends and/or family members who have children older than your child. Confide in parents you respect and who you believe have wisely raised their children. Hopefully, you will find that there are a few parents with whom you feel the freedom to fully express your concerns. Your Senior Parents are a good sounding board and will help you think through steps and strategies that have to do with helping your child feel better. These parents are a great support for you as you continue to stay one step ahead of what your child is learning about herself as she copes with Fibromyalgia.

The Body

The pediatrician or general practitioner (GP) needs to be someone with whom you can be fully honest. And be a person who is able to give you and your child the time needed so there is no feeling of being rushed in and out of the doctor's office. Your Senior Parents are a good referral source if you do not feel that you are currently receiving that kind of care.

The Western medical model is one that comes from a "let's rule things out" perspective. It is a pretty linear way of working, but it keeps a good focus so that you do not end up chasing your tails and going nuts with diagnostic tests. At the same time, it is reasonable to discuss tests with your child's doctor that you have researched via reputable sources like the Mayo Clinic or John Hopkins Medical Center, among others. When the doctor wants to draw blood and run blood work tests to rule out issues, you may want to make a suggestion or request something that the doctor might not be looking for at the moment.

When the various tests have been run and results are negative but the symptoms are still present, your child will—most likely—be referred to a pediatric rheumatologist. Remember to make sure that the rheumatologist receives a full copy of your child's pediatric records before the first appointment in order to avoid any unnecessary testing.

THE MIND

Most medical professionals will agree that there is a "mood component" to Fibromyalgia especially in children and teens who have been under stress. The what, why, how, and where of any stress in your child's life is important to observe. Documenting the stressful events that she has survived is helpful. Provide your doctor with a list of family events, such as divorce, death, or trauma. For each event give her age and circumstances surrounding the event.

Wherever possible, helping your child or teenager make the changes needed to lower the stressors in her life is the way to go. This may take the form of becoming more involved for the time being with her academic life, her home life, and/or her social life.

Specifically, help your child simplify her daily activities (much in the same way you learned to simplify your own).

Another area to watch is how your child views or thinks about herself. Rather than focus on the negative feelings that naturally arise, help her to see and express things in a more positive way. Above all, remember that you are her best teacher. By your modeling a positive mental attitude and approach to challenges, your child will hopefully do the same.

The emotional/mental health of parent and child may need to be addressed by a professional. These services may be provided privately, and some insurance companies may or may not cover the full cost. Or, there are clinics and service centers run by the state departments of mental health which offer professional counseling and support services. There are also foundations and private agencies offering similar services. The social work department at local hospitals is another source of referrals.

THE SPIRIT

It is important to laugh and to have fun. We have fallen into a belief that academic and extracurricular excellence guarantees our children success in life. Dr. Veronica Downes is an Irish general practitioner who has specialized in Fibromyalgia treatment. She and many other healthcare providers have noticed that this current lack of healthy fun and joy has had a negative impact on our children's lives—so much so that children are sick from so much pressure and over–stimulation. That is when we, the parents, need to use our sense of humor. Our example of being light and positive people, expressing our true nature, will guide our children back to their own joy–filled nature.

When we look at a nine–month old infant, we are looking at our true nature. What we see is a person who is in love with her world. If she is uncomfortable or hungry, she lets everyone know about it immediately. Helping our children and ourselves return to that joyful place is the name of the game. Putting a positive spin on all that life hands us is key in helping ourselves and our child live successfully. Look upon Fibromyalgia as a life lesson that teaches you to be fully present in the moment. Combine that feeling with a positive outlook, and you will help yourself as much as you will help your child or teenager.

School

The school system is stretched to its limits dealing with loads of issues and regulations about seat time in class, grades, lack of adequate teaching and administrative staff, and funding. Meanwhile your child has been missing days of school due to pain and discomfort which all contribute to her state of mind, motivation, and attitude. There are "Family Resource Centers" in many communities, and their purpose is to assist families coping with challenges, such as educating a child with a diagnosis and/ or a disability. Find one in your area and become familiar with what services they will offer you. They are, at the very least, a great resource of information and often will be able to help you complete any applications or forms that the school system requires to ensure that your child or teenager gets the assistance she needs.

It is important to become familiar with any program for which your child may be eligible due to her extended absences. Some school boards have a "homebound' and/or "intermittent homebound" program that will assist children with any diagnosis to receive extra tutoring. These sorts of programs are crucial to your child who is attempting to stay at her grade level. Bear in mind the school may not openly advertise that this kind of assistance is available. It is up to you to be one chapter ahead of the class and find out what kind of help is out there from your local Board of Education and/or the Family Resource Center. The earlier you get involved with the process, the easier it will be for your child and your family. Some programs will allow your child to come and go to school (while missing a class here and there) and will do so without docking her the required seat time as designated by your local Board of Education.

In America, children with a diagnosis may get assistance through a 504 Plan which is meant to protect the disabled and make accommodations at school. If that does not help, then an Individualized Education Plan (IEP) might be indicated. IEPs are for those children or teenagers whose disability impedes the learning process. Parents ought to email the principal and the special education department at the student's school and request their assistance. Documentation will be needed to address how the disability is impeding learning. Remember to include letters and reports from doctors in the documentation. An effective IEP should contain measurable and specific goals. In the case of Fibromyalgia, pro–social goals as well as functional goals need to be addressed.

Generally, the Guidance Department at the local school is not equipped to be of much help other than support. The Guidance Counselors are mostly there to provide a sort of catch–all safety net for all pupils whether they have behavioral problems or not and whether they do or do not have a diagnosis or an IEP. There is an excellent website, www.wrightslaw.com, that is a comprehensive resource on special education law and children and disabilities advocacy. Although this site addresses issues specific to the American educational system, there is much information here that is applicable internationally. A comparable international website is www.enfa-europe.eu, which organizes sister Fibromyalgia associations throughout Europe in order to raise awareness of, give voice to, and influence policy decisions on Fibromyalgia.

Once your child has been cleared for academic assistance via a homebound program, it is likely that her teachers will bend over backwards to keep your child current academically. Teachers are amazing people and usually are limited only by the bureaucracy in which they work. Emailing each teacher via group emails helps everyone stay in the loop. Remember to keep copies of all emails for future reference, if needed. If your child or teen has the energy to email her teachers (and you!), her teachers will be impressed by her focus and motivation. Creating this sort of communication between the school and the student helps eliminate misunderstandings down the line.

Working with her teachers and enlisting them to become her ally is a priority. Some teachers will be open to creating a study plan for your child and may explain what homework or lessons are in the works for the future. This kind of partnership between your child and her teachers will help her be better able to keep up with the school work when she has the energy. At the same time, it is important that you and the teachers work in concert to minimize the emotional pressure for your child as pressure equals stress. Communicating a logical study plan to your child which is attainable and realistic will work wonders in lowering her stress.

One of the most important things to keep in mind is that your child needs to socialize. She needs to be with her peers. Having her at home 24/7 is depressing to everyone. School is her world and she needs to be a part of it. The school, however, may want to keep her at home because it appears that she is missing "too much school and needs to rest up." It then is up to you to advocate her placement in a program which allows her to attend school as often as possible—even if it is for only a class or two a day. Unfortunately, without knowing the various programs that are available, your child might end up homebound when she was actually able to attend school some of the time.

CHAPTER 5

PLANNING FOR TODAY AND TOMORROW

Focus on Personal and Financial Resources

Ensuring Your Whole Family Wellness

As a mindful and common sense kind of parent, you will keep yourself centered as you go about the business of caring for your family. Part of that effort includes staying aware of the long term effects having a child or teen with Juvenile Fibromyalgia will have on the whole family. The day–to–day experience of living with any chronic illness engenders particular stressors within the family unit, and sometimes these overwhelming feelings can lead one or more of the family members to experience some degree of traumatic stress. Each family member needs to be made aware of, be on the lookout for, and actively seek to deal with the signs that can trigger feelings of stress, anger, fatigue, and impotence.

Studies of traumatic injury and the long term effects on both a child or teen and the family members suggest that 1–out–of–6 children and their parents experience significant after–effects, *i.e.* post–traumatic stress. Dr. Nancy Kassam–Adams, a psychologist who is the director of the Center for Pediatric Traumatic Stress at

Children's Hospital of Philadelphia, is the lead author of a review on post–traumatic stress in both children and parents after a child was injured. Her study reports that both children and parents may have intrusive and distressing memories and dreams, or continue to avoid people or places that evoke the circumstances of the injury, and may struggle with mood problems, including depression. One conclusion of the study is that if left untreated, the injured child's emotional and physical recovery may be compromised. Another implication is that the wellness of the family unit also becomes compromised. Finally, it speaks to the importance of knowing the signs which indicate extra help and support is needed to maintain a sense of well being.

Signs and symptoms include nightmares, dry mouth, panicky feelings, anxiety, depression, and flashbacks to previous trauma. Also be aware if someone is isolating. An example of isolating would be if you and/or a family member are avoiding situations that used to give pleasure, like meeting up with friends or looking forward to seeing a popular movie. Sinking moods that keep anyone in the family feeling down for a few weeks may be a sign that depression is settling in.

The intention of *Your Child's Well-Being - Juvenile Fibromyalgia* is to inform you of several techniques and attitudes that, if adopted, will help to prevent or combat traumatic stress. The most important piece to learn is that you actively need to provide self–care for yourself and teach it to your children. If, however, the signs of post–traumatic stress continue for more than a few weeks, then getting help from your doctor or family counselor is the way to go.

MANAGING YOUR FINANCIAL WELLNESS

Raising any child means there will be an exchange of monies for school uniforms, footballs, piano lessons, school books, and more. The same is true for raising a child diagnosed with Juvenile Fibromyalgia Syndrome.

Hopefully, you have in place an organized financial plan for paying your bills and saving for the future. Perhaps you even have a diversified investment portfolio. Think of the expenses you incur for your child or teen as an investment in her well being. As soon as you can, you will likely want to create or adjust your financial planning to accommodate the additional financial responsibilities. Start by keeping track of the receipts—for supplements, medications, heating pads, and the like—as well as medical receipts and/or papers concerning medical tests or evaluations from each of your healthcare practitioners. Having these documents organized and accessible will also help when preparing your tax return.

If you need to create a system, one simple solution is to purchase a three–ring notebook and a box of plastic sleeves that will fit in the binder. (Your office supply store will likely call them "sheet protectors.") Then, all you will need to do is slip the receipts into a sleeve. Make sure that dates are noted and add any other relevant comment that may prove useful in the future. You will figure out whether your folder works best for you in chronological order or by practitioner. The main thing is to keep it simple so that you will be inclined to stay current with organizing these papers.

How to Pay?

Learning that you have a child who has significant health requirements may lead to unexpected expenses added to your household budget. You may have some sort of health care coverage, in the form of insurance, which will help defray some percentage of the medical expenses. While your plan may include prescription medications, it may or may not cover the specific medications your child will require. You may even need to obtain a health insurance policy specifically designed for your child. Even with health insurance, your child's health care will require effort to manage costs.

In order to smooth out your expenses, you might contact the billings manager with each of your child's medical providers and work out a payment plan. Most countries abide by "good faith" agreements which allow you to negotiate a monthly payment which is comfortable for you to manage.

Here's a tip if you are dealing with a large facility's billing department. If the person who you are calling is kind, patient, and understanding, carry on and talk to them. If that person does not seem friendly, make an excuse to get off the phone and say that you will call them back later. Then phone the department again and see if you get a more understanding person. The point is that it is easier to negotiate with someone who will respectfully understand your situation than someone who does not. Often times, the greater empathy that is shown to you will result in a more manageable good faith agreement. And by explaining your personal financial circumstances and responsibilities, the billing department staff will get a realistic understanding on how the provided health care services will be paid back.

Another approach to financing your child's care in a medical setting is to contact the social work department. Usually the facility will have assigned a particular social worker to pediatric rheumatology cases with whom you may consult about available avenues to help manage your finances. The social worker will be able to explain the pros and cons of the available resources and help you through the application process.

Stress about finances is one of the leading causes of arguments in any family. It's always a wise idea for parents to sit down regularly and go over the budget and assess the financial situation. If you are a single parent, do the same thing: have a meeting with yourself every two or three weeks to review your financial binder and refresh your memory of what is current; what must be addressed in the short term—like calls to be made, checks to be written, and appointments to be kept.

Found Money?

An alternative way of getting medical care for your child or teen is checking around to see if there are any Fibromyalgia medical studies for children or adolescents at the medical centers in your area. Sometimes, the medical facility conducting studies on or about physical therapy, mindfulness training, and medication trials, need participants. Often, part of the research protocols for these studies will include free medical examinations and medication.

Should your child or teen be enrolled in a research study, make sure you are made aware of all the procedures and medications. If you disagree with any of the protocols in the study and choose to withdraw your child from the study, contact one of the researchers and set up a meeting to discuss your concerns.

CHAPTER 6

COMING THROUGH TO THE OTHER SIDE

Three Memoirs

The following histories are a compilation of issues, characteristics, and stories told to us over the years in our private practices. All identities and identifying factors have been changed so that privacy and confidentiality remain intact.

BETTY'S STORY

Learning to live with body pain started when I was first told at age 10 that the continual pain in my legs was "growing pains." That didn't make much sense to me because all of my friends were growing and were not complaining about "growing pains." No one took my pain seriously. All my mother would suggest was that I take a warm bath. I'm sure I was the only child I knew who spent so much time in the bath tub. I still have "growing pains" but now, fifty years later, it's called "restless leg syndrome." It feels exactly the same way now that it felt then: prickly sensations which caused me to move my legs all the time or need to walk around. It is especially painful at night when I'm trying to get to sleep. Actually, when I look back, I believe my current sleep problem started with these "growing pains" and has continued to this very day. I guess this pain was the first Fibromyalgia symptom I learned to live with.

Another symptom I struggle with is a serious sleep problem. Just as when I was a child, I still take warm baths each night before bedtime to calm the leg pain and movement. I remember finding it difficult to fall asleep on many childhood nights. And after I would finally manage to get to sleep, I'd often wake up many times either due to anxiety or bad dreams. I could not turn over and go back to sleep like most people would have done. I would actually have to get up and move. I usually ended up walking around the house all night long.

My inability to sleep left me extremely fatigued, and the fatigue quickly started affecting my school work and socializing with my friends. I remember days at a time trying to stay alert from what I now know to call "fibro fog." Looking back, the amazing thing to me is that no one seemed to notice when I was in a stupor. Somehow, I managed to go on with my high school life, even though I sometimes had to "will" myself to push through the day.

While in high school, I was thrown from a horse and spent a week in traction in the hospital. This experience left me with a "bad back" and lots of pain. I figured it was something I inherited because both parents had back problems. Here I am, supposedly a normal teenager, suffering the pain from restless leg syndrome; a sleep deprivation problem resulting in major fatigue; and now a back problem. All I could do was take aspirin like my parents did.

Over time, the mounting pain and lack of sleep caused me to become more anxious and depressed, so at age fifteen my doctor put me on Librium. It didn't stop the body pain and stiffness, but it did ease my anxiety and lift my depression. Then, right before graduating from high school, I was in a car accident, which stressed out my back again. One more thing to deal with. The best my doctor could do was prescribing muscle relaxants for spasms.

I finished high school and went on with my life having to be very conscious of my body and taking care of myself. I would often have what I now know to call "Fibromyalgia flare–ups," which was really a total melt down from the pain. I would (and still do) have to stay in bed for maybe a week. I had almost learned to manage and live with the pain and all the other symptoms that developed, when I was in another more serious car accident. This time I spent six weeks in hospital, again in traction, undergoing treatment for whip–lash and trauma to my lower back. This experience was a turning point. I had to spend years in physical therapy and began wearing a back brace as needed. I guess it helped. Without it, I expect I would have ended up permanently disabled.

The question that faced me was, how was I going to deal with a broken body, lots of pain and constant stiffness for the rest of my life? I decided I really had to take charge and search out some course of treatment or someone to help me. I began by consulting different doctors; each just wanted to give me medication for my symptoms. I decided I would be better off if I concentrated on one thing, to see if I could at least address and resolve one issue. My back pain seemed the logical place to start. I went to a major muscular skeletal hospital in New York City for consultation. I was told that I had a herniated disc in my lower back that needed surgery. I agreed to the surgery expecting to get some relief. I did get some relief from one kind of pain, but as you might guess, I ended up with a different kind of pain.

After that, I went to other doctors seeking relief for all the other symptoms. With no satisfactory results and still no actual diagnosis, I consulted a rheumatologist who diagnosed me with Lupus. I also learned I had Osteoarthritis. Following more tests and consultations, the diagnosis was changed to Fibromyalgia, which no one seemed to know much of anything about and largely dismissed it as depression. I tried everything the doctors suggested—medication, physical therapy, swimming, acupuncture, massage, chiropractic treatments. None of these helped and sometimes it made my pain worse. By this time, I was ready to give up on ever finding a way out of what seemed like an endless, circular journey.

I decided to go back to my internist and together work to find the right treatments for my symptoms. By this time, he was aware of the Fibromyalgia diagnosis and did everything he could to help me. One day, out of nowhere, he recommended I go to a sleep clinic. So I went. I told the doctor that this was my last attempt to find help and that I had gone to every specialist possible without gaining results. I spent two nights at the clinic and at the end of the two–day testing, I was told I had restless leg syndrome and sleep apnea, both caused by Fibromyalgia. The tests also showed that I never went into REM sleep and probably never had, since I had obviously been suffering with restless leg syndrome since childhood. Medication was prescribed to regulate my sleeping pattern, and after about six months, I started feeling better and experienced less body pain. Unfortunately there were side effects from this medication which caused other symptoms, so I stopped taking it and went back to my internist, this time armed with all the information I had gained from the sleep clinic.

Together, my internist and I figured out which medications I could tolerate without side effects to treat my symptoms. I'm actually still following this regimen today. It is not perfect, by any means. I do have less pain and because of that I can sleep better, which means less fatigue and fewer flare–ups. I was fifty–five years old when I reached this breakthrough. Now, years later, I'm still treating the same old familiar symptoms with basically the same medications for symptoms I was given from the time I was a teenager in high school, before anyone knew anything about "Fibromyalgia."

I have learned a lot about my body and how I need to take care of myself through this journey. Having a sense of humor contributed positively to maintaining my resilience and motivation. I have also learned how medications and Fibromyalgia affect my body. I mostly feel "OK" these days—until I have a fibro flare–up, and then I just ride it out doing all the things that have helped me in the past.

I look back over the last 50 years or so and realize most of my life has been spent trying to feel better and seek out answers to a very elusive disorder. Given all that I've been through, it did not surprise me to learn that no two cases of Fibromyalgia are ever alike. This is my story of Fibromyalgia. My experience of repetitive physical and emotional trauma definitely is the foundation for Fibromyalgia Syndrome becoming a physical disorder. It's been a long, confusing, frustrating, lonely journey. Today I am grateful that I feel better than I ever have felt before, and that I have far fewer flare–ups because I've learned how to manage my Fibro. Oh, how I wish my parents would have had a book like your's when I was ten years old.

LAURA'S STORY

Sometimes it pays to be someone who is impatient for a solution. Many times, since my child's diagnosis, dealing with her symptoms, the repercussions at home, and at school has been a pain in the neck. The whole time I was looking for answers as to why my child seemed to be ill all the time. "Fibromyalgia" never crossed my mind. I had never even heard of it until a friend suggested that I should explore the possibility of Fibromyalgia. Once I had a word, I began reading up on the symptoms and all the treatments I could find. Sometimes, I just got overwhelmed, and sometimes the information just didn't seem right. All I wanted was to get back some semblance of a normal family life and help my child to feel better.

One of the things my husband and I learned is that our daughter's pre–diagnostic history of Fibromyalgia is a fairly average one. Starting when she was about fifteen, she began coming down with one virus after another. She had been under more stress than is normal for a teenager and ended up being treated for mononucleosis that Spring. The following November, she had had an operation to repair a deviated septum to help her breathe more easily. Viruses continued to be a recurring problem over the next two years.

Her pediatrician basically treated her symptoms as they came up, prescribing things like bed rest, acetaminophen, and gargling with warm salt water for the sore throats. I realized at a certain point after the viruses kept coming back that my child needed consistency and to see the same pediatrician with each office visit rather than being rotated through the group medical practice. I knew that was the only way we would have a chance to figure out why she was not fully recovering.

The longer my child's symptoms persisted, the more of a mystery they remained. After a battery of tests and blood work that didn't tell us anything new but did rule out Lupus and Multiple Sclerosis among other possibilities, her pediatrician referred her to a pediatric rheumatologist. Unfortunately, this doctor could not see my child for five months, so I decided to use that time and find other ways to help her deal with her pain, fatigue, headaches, stomach aches, sore throats, and sleeping issues that had been going on for so long.

I should perhaps offer a little history. My husband and I are two older parents raising an only child. When we were given the opportunity to relocate from New York City to Europe, we decided to jump on it because we believed that in Europe our child would get an excellent education in a more relaxed environment. She did get an excellent education. What we didn't expect was how much of an outsider she would be in her new school. She had to work really hard to make friends with the other children. An additional change that we didn't clearly anticipate was the different climate. Where we lived was much damper than New York City. During the first six months, our child needed antibiotics three times for chest infections.

Since I had always been careful with and concerned about taking antibiotics, I had developed an interest in homeopathy. The healing treatments I had tried over the years, such as acupuncture for aches and pains, along with energetic healing treatments, helped me in a lot of ways. So, I started introducing my child to homeopathic remedies at about age ten. The homeopath in our village did help our daughter build up her physical strength. However, she still missed at least twenty days of school every year because of viruses, colds and sore throats. The homeopath was terrific in helping my daughter to quickly get through all of these childhood illnesses. Without homeopathy who knows what her health would have been like in such a damp and wet climate.

After living abroad for nine years, it was time to return to America. Our daughter had been accepted to a high school for the arts and we were all thrilled that she had such an opportunity. However, this big change was further complicated by my staying behind for the year—continuing to work in order to insure that we had a steady source of income "in case" the plan to move wasn't going to work. My husband and I thought that my frequent visits to our new home would be enough emotional support for the three of us to help sustain us through the stress of such a big move. In hindsight, I realize that this was too stressful a path for our family.

When our daughter was fourteen years old, I decided to start taking her to an acupuncturist who recommended a weekly prescribed mix of Chinese herbs as per her changing symptoms. (We had now moved to America and there were no homeopaths where we lived.) I have never had a keen interest in cooking, but I instinctively knew I should be paying more attention to her diet. (The acupuncturist had taught me that sugar was definitely something to rule out of her food regime.) The nutritionist I went to helped me learn to cook using organically grown foods and non–dairy products. We found that this simple switch did make a noticeable difference.

It wasn't until we were finally able to consult with the pediatric rheumatologist that we got a definitive diagnosis of Fibromyalgia. Having the diagnosis helped a lot, but it also kind of threw us into new uncharted territory. Many times, every flare–up felt like we were thrown back to square one, and it often felt that we'd never be able to come out the other side.

Now that our daughter is off at college, our support is no longer needed on a daily basis. I am grateful to have found some paths that helped make managing Fibromyalgia easier for both my daughter and my family. Finding a path was not without cost. I had to give up my idea of a tidy little life and become an expert on what would be best for our daughter who was living with the rollercoaster of Fibromyalgia symptoms. At the same time, I still had to make a living, stay connected to my husband and manage my role as a parent.

Yet, I gained something, too. I learned that I needed to mind myself, to take a step back and start to take care of me. If I didn't, I wouldn't be of help anyone. Not to my child, not to my husband, not to my livelihood. I learned to make peace with my "new normal" and call a truce with this thing called Fibromyalgia.

Tom's Story

I first came to see my therapist for help dealing with frequent panic attacks. I told her how I had been on five different antidepressants and/or anti–anxiety medications over time and how, more recently, no medication was able to stop or prevent my having these attacks.

My goal in seeking counseling was to find a way to deal with these panic attacks and to become more independent. The work I started to do with my therapist began to focus around my life experiences and primarily concentrated on events from my childhood. I grew up in an English village south of London, the youngest of three children in a middle–income home. It was idyllic in a way, as my childhood was busy and fun because most of my family—grandparents, aunts, uncles, and cousins—lived in the same village. All except one uncle, who had moved to Chicago before I was born.

I say my childhood was "idyllic in a way" because the absence of that uncle was deeply felt by my parents and grandparents and other aunts and uncles. The sentiment only worsened when that uncle died in a car accident. I was eight years old at the time, and I clearly remember the dark mood of my parents and extended family after that. About a year later, my beloved grandmother suffered a severe stroke and came to live with my family, and that further altered familiar patterns and routines.

A couple of years after my grandmother came to live with us, I began experiencing muscle aches, frequent colds, upset stomachs, and had difficulty sleeping. My mother and the family GP did what they could to ease my symptoms, but nothing seemed to put me right. I began missing many school days and, consequently, fell behind academically. Tension at home became more and more noticeable, as now my mother and father had not only my elderly grandmother in need of constant care, but a young teenager who also required special attention.

I barely managed to scrape by academically and had to stop participating in sports at age sixteen due to muscle pain and extreme fatigue. During my secondary school years and between visits to the GP, I became aware of various alternative health care providers and began to seek advice from some. The herbs, teas, and other suggestions they offered were able to provide temporary relief. Nothing I tried provided long term results or restored my energy or kept me pain free.

Then, in my final year of secondary school, my symptoms grew to such extent that I was confined to my bed for the majority of the year. This development added a new symptom: chronic depression. My parents and I consulted many, many medical specialists during that very bad period of my life. I was put through many different diagnostic tests, all of which were inconclusive and led to ever higher levels of stress around the home. Not long thereafter is when I first began to experience multiple panic attacks which compelled me to withdraw from school before the Christmas Holidays in my final year.

The following summer, a new rheumatologist diagnosed me as suffering from Fibromyalgia. This rheumatologist prescribed exercise, counseling, and a low dose of amitriptyline to help me sleep which helped some of the time. For the next ten years thereafter, I consulted several counselors and learned new ways of managing my pain. I had to change medications when they no longer worked, for example, and I would have to give up any exercise regime whenever the discomfort and pain became too much.

Through psychotherapy, I began to develop a deeper understanding of my history. I began to feel better about myself and gained perspective about the life events my family and I had experienced. My therapist has taught me relaxation techniques, and I can use them to put myself into a relaxed state at will. The techniques have also helped me feel secure in my own power and given me the awareness required to monitor my tension levels.

I also learned CBT (Cognitive Behavioural Therapy) and practiced it to change the ways I thought and spoke in order to reflect a positivity that had not been there before. I learned more about how positive thoughts and ways of speaking rewire one's brain so as to not dip into depressive thinking. A couple of months into this counseling work, my panic attacks began to subside dramatically. My therapist recommended I seek a second opinion from a psychiatrist more experienced in Fibromyalgia and related disorders. This psychiatrist impressed me with a greater understanding of my situation. Adjustments in my medication brought about more positive changes, yet every several months its effects seemed to plateau. Currently, I am taking a medication that is helpful.

I started exploring alternative healthcare providers. I concentrated on learning about ways of moving my body that helped restore my strength. Some practices I liked and some I didn't. In particular I found value and benefit in certain yoga postures specific to Fibromyalgia. I discovered feeling better after changing to a gluten–free, sugar–free, and vegan diet. I also got a lot of benefit from mindfulness meditation training as well as NLP [Neuro Linguistic Programming] which is a method of positively reframing thoughts.

Managing my Fibromyalgia is a constant effort and not always easy, but it has gotten better after coming to rely upon certain modifications. I still live at home with an elder sister and my parents, but I am now able to drive which was an impossibility before. Being aware of my thought patterns has increased my energy and positivity throughout the day. My pain and fatigue levels have decreased by what seems like 80%, and I am looking forward to finding a career that is interesting and does not adversely affect my health. I know I have not "gotten rid" of Fibromyalgia, and I am thankful for having the skills that allow me to cope better than ever.

Afterword

Parents are amazing people. They will go to the ends of the earth to help their children. They will trawl the Internet into the late hours of the night looking for information to make sense out of what ails their child. They are the first and best advocates for their child. To each of you parents who are caring for a child with Fibromyalgia, we hope you will carry these few words of advice with you:

First, it is important that you understand what Fibromyalgia is, how it affects your child, your family, and how to take care of yourself so that you can take care of your child.

Second, how you care for yourself—so that you remain vital and connected at home, at work, and in your community—will be the best example for your child to learn how to take care of herself.

Yes, you may feel that you, too, are "coming through to the other side," as the life stories in the previous chapter were titled. No matter where you are on your journey, whether you are just setting out or somewhere in the middle, you must trust that you will not always feel so adrift. You must have faith that your path toward that other side is right at your feet.

The moment of diagnosis may first register as shock, then fear. Fortunately, JFMS is not life–threatening. The shock will wear off and the fear will dissipate. In its place will be the wise, vigilant, and caring routine you and your family establish to manage her health at home, at school, and in her social life.

By not giving up, you kept your hope alive even though sometimes you didn't feel like it. The love of your child has made it possible for you to find everything that you needed to know. As a result, your family will have become much closer and will be enjoying each other even more.

Appendix

RESOURCES FOR FURTHER EXPLORATION

Books and Articles

Conquering Your Child's Chronic Pain, Lonnie K. Zeltzer, M.D. and Christina Blackett Schlank; William Morrow, an imprint of HarperCollins Publishers, Inc., © 2005. *This book is a comprehensive guide and resource listing to pediatric pain issues, including Juvenile Fibromyalgia.*

The Wizard's Wish, Brad Yates; Amazon's Create Space, © 2010. *This a very creative book which teaches the EFT/Tapping technique and is written for kids and "puts the power to feel good into kids' own hands—literally."*

"Juvenile Primary Fibromyalgia Syndrome: A Clinical Study of Thirty-three Patients and Matched Normal Controls," Dr. Muhammed Yunus, M.D. and Dr. Alfonse Masi, M.D., *Arthritis Rheum*, February 1985. *This paper is the first document to establish criteria for diagnosing Fibromyalgia and later adopted by the American College of Rheumatology.*

"Juvenile Primary Fibromyalgia Syndrome," Eileen R Giardino, RN, MSN, PhD, FNP-BC, ANP-BC; edited by Lawrence K. Jung, M.D., published at http://emedicine.medscape.com/article/1006715-overview and updated on 15 October, 2013. *Article provides a comprehensive and concise discussion of Juvenile Primary Fibromyalgia Syndrome.*

"Why Skeptics Love to Hate Homeopathy," Amy L. Lansky, Ph.D., republished (with permission) at www.myranissen. com/blog/why-skeptics-love-to-hate-homeopathy. *This is a thorough and professional article explaining homeopathy.*

"The Boy With a Thorn in His Joints," Susannah Meadows, *The New York Times Magazine*, 3 February 2013, pp. 32–36, 46. *This article chronicles one family's experience in balancing home, school, and social life after one child was diagnosed with a chronic illness.*

WEBSITES AND BLOGS

The following list gives you a head start on searching the Internet for information and resources. Explore any or all of those on this list, or conduct your own Google search. Any website will probably offer some kernel of information that may resonate with you and/or your child. As you use the Internet, bear in mind a couple of caveats.

First, many websites are not regularly updated. Often, websites spring up and actively and passionately disseminate information and offer support. Then, over time, the site's editor(s) may run out of new information or sources to share, and the website becomes inactive. Just remember to ask yourself, "When was this information published? How current is it?"

Second, consider the source. Like with other medical conditions, healthcare and pharmaceutical companies use the Internet and social media to promote their companies' own agenda along with providing information to the consumer. Getting a second opinion or finding independent confirmation is always a good practice.

Medical Centers which host Juvenile Fibromyalgia clinics

www.childrenshospital.org/health-topics/conditions/pediatric-Fibromyalgia-and-musculoskeletal-pain: Boston Children's Hospital is one of the largest pediatric medical centers in the United States offering a complete range of health care services for children from birth through 21 years of age and setting the pace in pediatric research by identifying treatments and therapies for many debilitating diseases.

www.chop.edu: The Children's Hospital of Philadelphia (CHOP) has been in the forefront in pediatric medicine since 1855, fostering medical discoveries and innovations that in pediatric healthcare which have repeatedly earned it recognition as one of the nation's best children's hospitals.

www.cincinnatichildrens.org/service/p/pain/services/pain-management-clinic/: Established in 1883, Cincinnati Children's offers comprehensive clinical services, from treatments for rare and complex conditions to well–child care, through fully integrated, globally recognized research, education, and innovation.

www.healthcare.ucla.edu/pedspain: The UCLA Children's Pain and Comfort Care Program (CPCCP) is dedicated to alleviating pain and other causes of distress for children from birth to young adulthood and focuses on providing care that improves the quality of life for both patients and families while also promoting an understanding of best practices in pediatric pain management and palliative care.

Fibromyalgia Associations and Directories

www.fmaaware.org: The National Fibromyalgia Association, a world–wide support organization founded by Lynne K. Matallana in 1997, is dedicated to sharing all the most important information on Fibromyalgia and related topics.

www.afsafund.org: The American Fibromyalgia Syndrome Association (AFSA) is a nonprofit organization dedicated to funding research that accelerates the pace of medical discoveries which hopefully will improve the quality of life for Fibromyalgia patients; the site explains Fibromyalgia and lists resources.

www.nfmcpa.org: The National Fibromyalgia & Chronic Pain Association unites patients, policy makers and healthcare, medical, and scientific communities to transform lives and end chronic pain conditions by promoting early diagnosis, driving scientific research for a cure and facilitating research into the treatment for Fibromyalgia and chronic pain.

www.enfa-europe.eu: The European Network of Fibromyalgia Associates organizes sister Fibromyalgia associations throughout Europe to raise awareness of, give voice to, and influence policy decisions on Fibromyalgia.

www.farny.org: The Fibromyalgia Association of Rochester New York (FARNY) is dedicated to meeting the needs of individuals diagnosed with Fibromyalgia by supporting, educating and informing patients, families, professionals, and the public concerning the nature of Fibromyalgia.

www.fmscommunity.org: The Fibromyalgia Community offers a comprehensive overview of services, support, information, and materials to help the public gain an understanding of Fibromyalgia.

General Forums

www.nlm.nih.gov/medlineplus/Fibromyalgia.html: Sponsored by the United States National Institutes of Health, MedlinePlus communicates free, reliable and up–to–date information on health and wellness issues including information on drugs and supplements or the meanings of words; the URL shown opens to the page on Fibromyalgia.

www.nccih.nih.gov: The National Center for Complementary and Alternative Medicine (NICAM), a department within the U.S. National Institutes of Health (NIH), conducts and supports research into and provides information about complementary health products and practices.

www.kidshealth.org/parent/medical/bones/Fibromyalgia.html: A blog post written for parents and published by the Nemours Foundation which is committed to improving the health of children through family–centered children's hospitals and clinics, as well as world–changing research, education, and advocacy.

www.emedicine.medscape.com: Medscape, a subsidiary of WebMD Health Professional Network, provides clinicians and other healthcare professionals with the most timely, comprehensive, and relevant clinical information to improve patient care.

www.fibroblog.org: This site is labeled as a resource for everything about Fibromyalgia; note that while some good information can be found here, the most recent posting was in June 2011.

www.b12patch.com/blog/Fibromyalgia/100-best-sites-for-Fibromyalgia-or-chronic-fatigue-information/: In May 2011, this list of 100 blogs on Fibromyalgia and Chronic Fatigue Syndrome, compiled by Vita Sciences, maker of the B12 patch, was posted in honor of that year's Fibromyalgia Awareness Week.

www.nhs.uk/Conditions/Fibromyalgia/Pages/Treatment.aspx: The National Health System of the United Kingdom (NHS) is a vast online encyclopedia on health, services, care, and headlines; this link leads to a very comprehensive and supportive site for Fibromyalgia.

www.fmauk.org: Fibromyalgia Association UK is a registered, all–volunteer charity which operates as a signpost to information and resources for people who are affected by Fibromyalgia; a recent search of the site found seven articles regarding Juvenile Fibromyalgia.

www.livestrong.com: Livestrong.com is the definitive destination for people who want to feel empowered through food and fitness because eating well and staying active are critical components in preventing illness; searching the site for "Fibromyalgia" yields over 1,400 listed results, including research articles regarding diet (foods to avoid, going gluten–free), medications, supplements, and fitness among other topics.

www.ukFibromyalgia.com: UK Fibromyalgia is an online magazine providing an independent voice for all Fibromyalgia sufferers in the United Kingdom; specifically, www.ukFibromyalgia.com/advice/fm-in-children.html discusses Juvenile Fibromyalgia while www.ukFibromyalgia.com/fm-resources.html offers an extensive list of clinics, charities, associations, and other resources.

www.Fibromyalgia-symptoms.org/Fibromyalgia_children.html: Page describes Juvenile Fibromyalgia, its treatment and offers a few tips for parents on this site which is dedicated to informing readers about important health issues, especially those related to the well-being of women and providing accurate, up-to -date information on Fibromyalgia.

www.meetup.com: Meetup is the world's largest network of local groups and lists over 100 support communities for Fibromyalgia and chronic pain.

www.facebook.com: Many groups and organizations, such as the National Fibromyalgia Association, share information and promote their activities on Facebook.

Alternative Therapies, Associations and Directories

www.bradyates.net: Brad Yates' main website promoting the Emotional Freedom Technique (EFT, a registered trademark of Gary Craig), which may be used to teach children how to tap away their pain and fatigue.

www.youtube.com/user/eftwizard?feature=chclk: Brad Yates' YouTube Channel offers hundreds of videos on how to use Tapping (EFT).

www.eftuniverse.com: Dawson Church, a master EFT practitioner, has a good list of research papers and projects regarding EFT under the section "EFT Essentials."

www.ncbtmb.org/tools/find-a-certified-massage-therapist: The National Certification Board for Therapeutic Massage and Bodywork (NCBTMB) offers a search directory for finding a certified massage therapist in the United States.

www.homeopathicdirectory.com: The Council for Homeopathic Certification (CHC) certifies individuals who meet and maintain a recognized standard of professional and ethical competence in classical homeopathy and assists the general public in choosing appropriately qualified homeopaths in the United States and Canada.

www.homeopathy-ecch.org/content/view/15/32/: The European Central Council of Homeopaths (ECCH) is an international council whose membership comprises established associations of professional homeopaths existing within the European Union and includes a searchable directory of homeopaths.

www.nccaom.org/find-a-nccaom-certified-practitioner: The National Certification Commission for Acupuncture and Oriental Medicine (NCCAOM®) establishes, assesses and promotes recognized standards of competence and safety in acupuncture and Oriental medicine for the protection and benefit of the public and includes a searchable directory to assist in the finding of a certified NCCAOM practitioner.

www.ehpa.eu: The European Herbal and Traditional Medicine Practitioners Association (EHTPA) comprises six professional herbal/traditional medicine associations with a membership of professional practitioners working across the United Kingdom and works closely with European Union herbal organizations and the World Health Organization (WHO) in setting standards worldwide.

www.tcmcentral.com: The Traditional Chinese Medicine Resource Center offers news and information regarding the theory and practice of Chinese medicine and acupuncture and includes a searchable worldwide directory of practitioners.

www.pocacoop.com/faq: The Peoples Organization of Community Acupuncturists is a 5,000+ member cooperative organization serving acupuncturists, patients, clinics, and supportive organizations; the frequently asked questions page does a good job of explaining what acupuncture is.

www.acmac.net: The Association of Community and Multibed Acupuncture Clinics (ACMAC) provides information and support to the acupuncture community and multibed acupuncture centers around the world and works in partnership with JCM and Balance Healthcare and Acupuncture CPD in the United Kingdom; Acuneeds in Australia; and POCA and Tanuwbian in the United States.

Legal Resource

www.wrightslaw.com: Wrightslaw is a resource for parents, educators, advocates, and attorneys offering information about special education law, education law, and advocacy for children with disabilities.

About The Authors

Christine Harris, LCSW, LISW-CP, DCC

 Christine Harris has been providing psychotherapeutic services for individuals (adults and children), couples and families for over 20 years either in a face-to-face setting or as a distance counselor using video-conferencing. In addition to maintaining a private practice, she has also worked as a consultant for a wide range of organizations including hospitals, senior citizen agencies, brain injury, and disability centers, pediatric care programs, and programs providing specialized care for challenging illnesses like HIV+, AIDS, and cancer.

Upon completion of her Master's of Social Work degree at New York University, Christine continued her traditional professional development by further studies in Family Therapy, Gestalt, Cognitive, Psychodynamic, Guided Imagery, Autogenic Relaxation, and Focusing.

To learn more about Christine and her work, visit www. ChristineHarrisTherapy.com and/or www.yourchildswellbeing.com.

Kay Prothro, LCSW–R, ACSW

 Kay Prothro has been working with patients and clients on human potential and human development issues for over 35 years. As a Menninger–trained psychotherapist in private practice in New York City, Kay specializes in working with Adults, Adult Development, and Couples Therapy. She has spearheaded many innovative health programs nationally for groups, families, couples, and individuals.

Kay works with her clients by focusing on finding strategies relating to mind-body-spirit wellness and healthy conscious living. Her primary areas of focus include interpersonal and family relationships, life–challenging illnesses, grief counseling, aging, life transitions, and stress management.

After completing The Menninger Post Graduate Fellowship Program, Kay furthered her education at the Institute for Life Coach Training and the Blanton–Peale Graduate Institute. She originally trained as a psycho–dynamic psychotherapist and has since become known for consolidating transpersonal, integral, and cognitive behavioral perspectives into her work.

To learn more about Kay and her work, visit www.JustImagineNYC.com and/or www.yourchildswellbeing.com.

ACKNOWLEDGMENTS

The authors wish to thank the families, children, and teens who shared their Fibromyalgia stories and wisdom. Also, our thanks for the guidance and support from Chris Deatherage, M.A., Dr. Veronica Downes, GP, Bridie Hackett, Chad Houfek, L.Ac., Susmita Kashikar-Zuck, Ph.D., Linda Lyons, Lic. Ac., Dip. Ac., Lynne Morrison, O.M.D., L.Ac., Kate Soudant, I.S.Hom., C.C.H., Brad Yates, Lonnie K. Zeltzer, M.D., and the Bergaust & Harris Families.

Printed in the United States
By Bookmasters

Your Child's Well-Being - Juvenile Fibromyalgia is a practical and uplifting resource guide for all parents and family members of children and teenagers who may be living with Fibromyalgia. Full of up-to-date information and guidance, this book will help you to successfully navigate the Fibromyalgia terrain.

ENDORSEMENTS FOR 'YOUR CHILD'S WELL-BEING - JUVENILE FIBROMYALGIA'

"This book is a 'must-read' for any parent of a child with widespread pain. We now know that a cluster of symptoms, such as pain, fatigue, mental fogginess, difficulty sleeping, anxiety, and depression, in any combination, are part of the fibromyalgia like syndrome. This book is easy to read and provides some important guides on how parents can help their child. I give it a strong recommendation!"

— **Lonnie Zeltzer, MD**
Director, Pediatric Pain and Palliative Care Program
Distinguished Professor of Pediatrics, Anesthesiology, Psychiatry and
Biobehavioral Sciences, David Geffen School of Medicine at UCLA

"Having a child diagnosed with Juvenile Fibromyalgia sometimes can be a long and confusing journey and this book is a truly empathic guide that should give parents and caregivers a sense of empowerment and hope. Most importantly, the authors have put together an easy-to-read book which offers practical support and resources for parents to get the best care for their child and assist their child to achieve a well-balanced life despite their symptoms. I would recommend it as a must-read for parents of teens with JFM."

— **Susmita Kashikar-Zuck, PhD**
Professor of Pediatrics and Licensed Psychologist
Cincinnati Children's Hospital Medical Center

"This is a great resource you've put together – well done! And thank you for including EFT/tapping as a tool that folks can use to help relieve both the physical and emotional discomfort faced by the children and the people who love them."

— **Brad Yates**, *Author of The Wizard's Wish*

U.S. $9.99
ISBN 978-1-5043-3925-4

50999

9 781504 339254

Balboa
PRESS
A DIVISION OF HAY HOUSE

Are you ready for your prayers to be answered?

Heal Your Mind
and Your Body
Will Heal,
— Book 1 —

A Book of Prayers

REV. DR. ALMA MARIE STEVENS